COOL CARS

McLAREN 720S

BY THOMAS K. ADAMSON

EPIC

BELLWETHER MEDIA ››› MINNEAPOLIS, MN

EPIC BOOKS are no ordinary books. They burst with intense action, high-speed heroics, and shadows of the unknown. Are you ready for an Epic adventure?

This edition first published in 2023 by Bellwether Media, Inc.

No part of this publication may be reproduced in whole or in part without written permission of the publisher. For information regarding permission, write to Bellwether Media, Inc., Attention: Permissions Department, 6012 Blue Circle Drive, Minnetonka, MN 55343.

Library of Congress Cataloging-in-Publication Data

LC record for McLaren 720S available at: https://lccn.loc.gov/2022020240

Text copyright © 2023 by Bellwether Media, Inc. EPIC and associated logos are trademarks and/or registered trademarks of Bellwether Media, Inc.

Editor: Kieran Downs   Designer: Jeffrey Kollock

Printed in the United States of America, North Mankato, MN

TABLE OF CONTENTS

LAUNCH MODE	4
ALL ABOUT THE 720S	6
PARTS OF THE 720S	12
THE FUTURE OF THE 720S	20
GLOSSARY	22
TO LEARN MORE	23
INDEX	24

LAUNCH MODE ≫

A McLaren 720S sits on an empty road. The driver presses the launch button. She steps on the gas pedal.

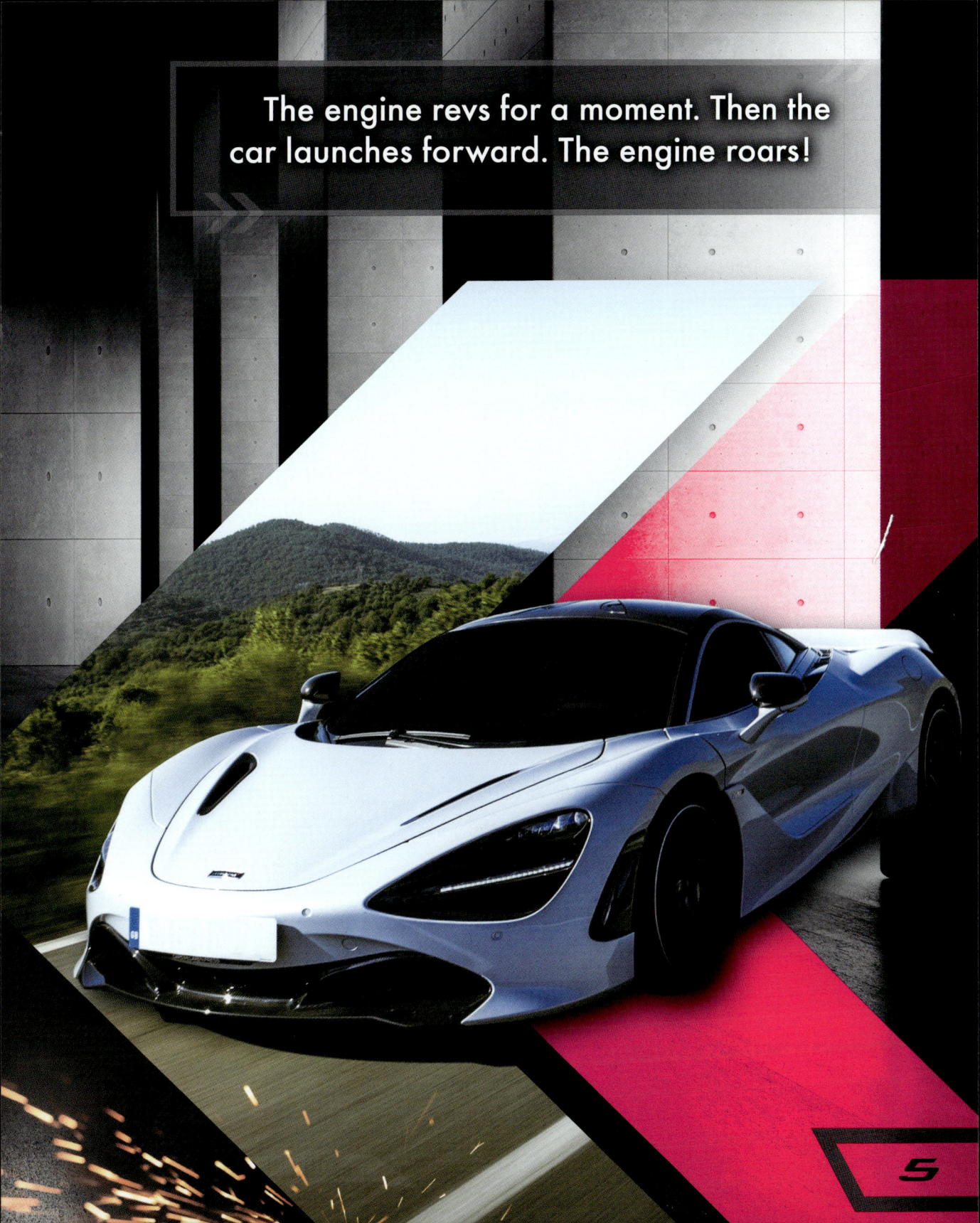

The engine revs for a moment. Then the car launches forward. The engine roars!

ALL ABOUT THE 720S

1960 FORMULA 1 RACE

McLaren started building race cars in the 1960s. McLarens are built at the McLaren Production Centre in England. This is also the home of their **Formula 1** racing team.

Famous McLarens include the 650S, the 570S, and the GT.

MCLAREN GT

RACING TO THE ROAD

McLaren's first road car was the M6GT. Only three of them were built!

📍 WHERE IS IT MADE?

WOKING, ENGLAND

EUROPE

McLaren first showed the 720S in 2017. It is faster than earlier McLaren cars. It is also more powerful.

2017 720S

The 720S is fast enough for racing. But it is comfortable enough for road driving.

The 720S is stylish. Its body features a lot of curves and swoops.

Every curve has a purpose. They help the car's **aerodynamics**. The shape helps the car slice through the air.

SPECIAL DOORS

The doors on the 720S open upward. The door handles are hidden!

720S BASICS

YEAR FIRST MADE 2017

COST starts at $301,500

HOW MANY MADE unknown

FEATURES

V8 engine

hidden air intakes

rear spoiler

PARTS OF THE 720S »

AIR INTAKES

The 720S has many hidden **air intakes**. These openings are in the doors, rear, and even in the headlights.

They channel air to the engine to keep it cool. They are hidden to make the car look smooth.

HEADLIGHT AIR INTAKES

The **V8 engine** in the 720S gets extra power from its **turbochargers**. These parts squeeze more air into the engine.

This allows more fuel to enter the engine. It gains more power without adding much more weight.

ENGINE SPECS

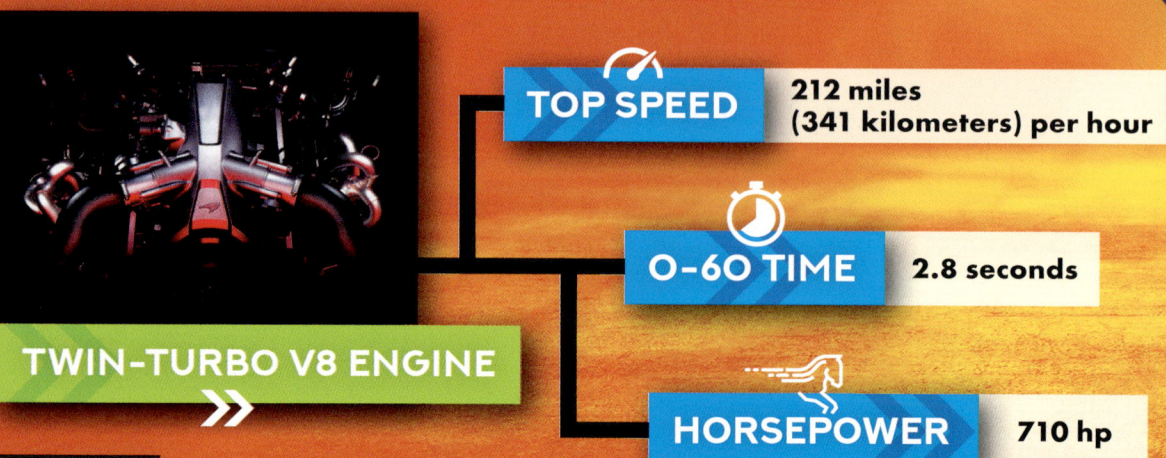

TWIN-TURBO V8 ENGINE

TOP SPEED — 212 miles (341 kilometers) per hour

0–60 TIME — 2.8 seconds

HORSEPOWER — 710 hp

The frame of the 720S is made of **carbon fiber** and **aluminum**. The materials are lightweight and strong.

LIGHTWEIGHT FRAME

SPOILER

A rear **spoiler** improves **downforce**. The car is easier to control at high speeds. The spoiler also pops up to help the car slow down.

The McLaren 720S Spider is a **convertible**. The roof takes only 11 seconds to open.

720S SPIDER

LIGHT ROOF

The Spider's roof is made of carbon fiber. It adds just 108 pounds (49 kilograms) to the car's weight.

SIZE CHART

WIDTH 76 inches (193 centimeters)

The Spider also features an **electrochromic** roof. The roof's window becomes shaded with the touch of a button.

ELECTROCHROMIC ROOF

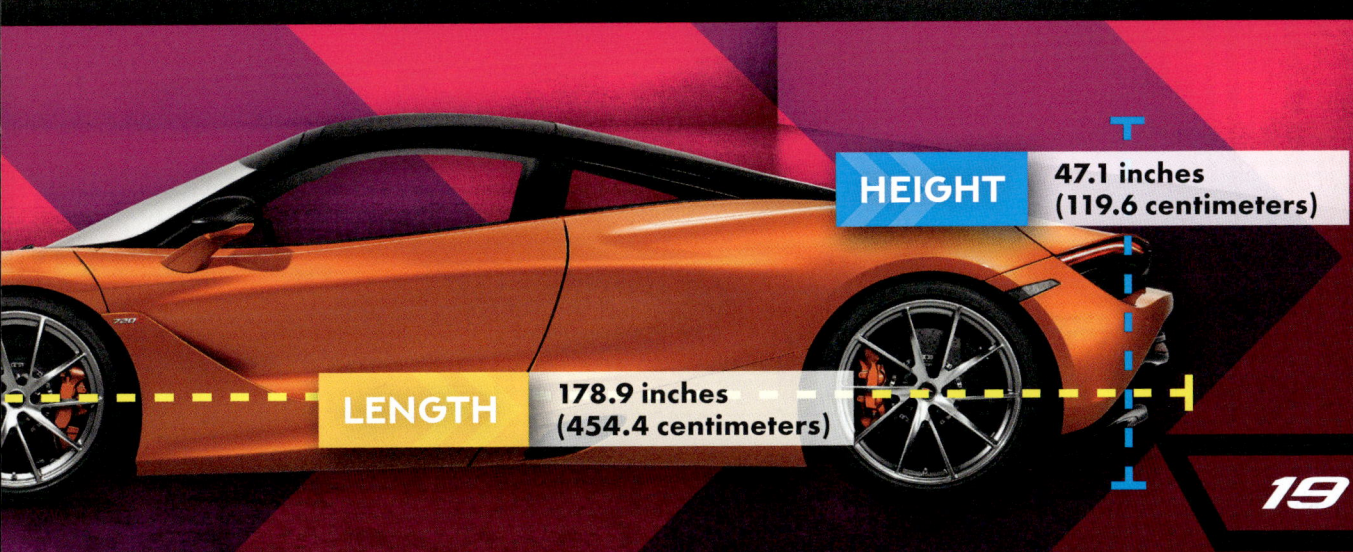

HEIGHT 47.1 inches (119.6 centimeters)

LENGTH 178.9 inches (454.4 centimeters)

THE FUTURE OF THE 720S

McLaren is still making the 720S. The company has also started making **hybrids**. An **electric car** is also in the works. McLaren will keep making cars for drivers to enjoy!

BENDING LIGHT

The headlights on the 720S move as the steering wheel turns. This makes it easier to see around curves.

GLOSSARY

aerodynamics—the system on a sports car that is designed to help it move through the air easily and quickly

air intakes—openings that air can flow into to help cool a car's engine

aluminum—a strong, lightweight material

carbon fiber—strong, lightweight fibers used to strengthen material

convertible—a car with a top that can be lowered or removed

downforce—a force that pushes down on a car

electric car—a car that does not need gas to run

electrochromic—able to change to be shaded

Formula 1—an international car racing series

hybrids—cars that use both a gasoline engine and an electric motor for power

spoiler—a part on the back of a car that helps the car grip the road

turbochargers—engine parts that force high-pressure air into the engine to create extra power

V8 engine—an engine with 8 cylinders arranged in the shape of a "V"

TO LEARN MORE

AT THE LIBRARY

Garstecki, Julia. *McLaren 720S*. Mankato, Minn.: Black Rabbit Books, 2020.

Murray, Julie. *McLaren F1*. Minneapolis, Minn.: Abdo Zoom, 2020.

Storm, Marysa. *Supercars*. Mankato, Minn.: Black Rabbit Books, 2020.

ON THE WEB

FACTSURFER

Factsurfer.com gives you a safe, fun way to find more information.

1. Go to www.factsurfer.com.

2. Enter "McLaren 720S" into the search box and click 🔍.

3. Select your book cover to see a list of related content.

INDEX

aerodynamics, 10
air intakes, 12, 13
aluminum, 16
basics, 11
body, 10
carbon fiber, 16, 18
company, 6, 7, 8, 20
convertible, 18
doors, 10, 12
downforce, 17
electric car, 20
engine, 5, 13, 14
engine specs, 14
Formula 1, 6
frame, 16
headlights, 12, 13, 21
history, 6, 7, 8
hybrids, 20
McLaren Production Centre, 6

models, 7, 8, 18, 19
racing, 6, 9
roof, 18, 19
size chart, 18–19
speed, 8, 9, 17
Spider, 18, 19
spoiler, 17
turbochargers, 14
Woking, England, 7

The images in this book are reproduced through the courtesy of: McLaren, front cover, pp. 1, 3, 4, 4-5, 7, 8-9 (right), 10-11, 11 (isolated, engine, intakes, spoiler), 12, 12-13, 13 (headlight), 14, 14-15, 16 (frame), 16-17, 17, 18, 18 (width), 18-19 (length), 19, 19 (roof), 20-21 (right); Bernard Cahier/ Getty Images, p. 6; i viewfinder, pp. 8-9 (left); PA Images/ Alamy, pp. 20-21.